Bloom
for Yourself II

Let go and grow

April Green

Also by April Green:

Bloom for Yourself

A few years ago, I fell apart. And in the process of building myself back up, I learned that you are allowed to leave some pieces behind—you are allowed to become the person you design yourself to be.

ॐ   ॐ   ॐ

A collection of notes, and poetic reflections, journaling how I learned to let go of everything holding me back in order to grow into the person I deserved to become.

Bloom for Yourself II is a book you can plant in your soul and return to each time you feel ready to let go and grow.

Cover Artwork:
Xavier Esclusa Trias
www.twopots-design.com
xevi@twopots-design.com

Handwritten Font:
Sam Parrett
www.setsailstudios.com

ISBN–13:978-1527230958
ISBN–10:1527230953

for tina. for you. for us.

🌿   🌿   🌿

wildflower—
keep unfolding
in front of their eyes.

(without apology)

April Green— Bloom for Yourself

let go

My dear reader

Before you even start thinking about letting go of the old life—before you allow the light to break free from heavy bones, fragile skin cast behind like shadow— please know that the vast and terrifying space of loss doesn't get narrower over time. It doesn't harden or collapse in on itself. It softens. Depending on what you allow in, it softens, and widens; becomes filled with beautiful memories, new life, magic.

If you place flowers there—they will keep blooming for you.

April Green

The exchange

Too often, we find so many things to worry about and fight against that we end up unable to even think about letting ourselves grow into all we deserve to become.

But growth just can't happen when you're holding onto the past; to fear, to secrets, to denial, or any other kind of resistance. For all of these things make moving forward impossible—like a ship trying to set sail while anchored to the shore.

Growth happens when your desire to grow becomes much stronger than your pain. It happens with the sudden realisation that you deserve more than what you're settling for. It happens in a moment—a moment that may have taken years to flutter quietly into the light of your awareness—but, it's a magical moment, an exchange; where your hands let go of all that they're holding, so they can grasp a fragment of air, an inhale, a miracle that changes everything.

April Green

Restoration

No-one ever tells you this: you are allowed to rebuild.

It's one of those things you work out for yourself when the walls start crumbling, and the words you scratched behind them start rising with the dust; when every inhale becomes a storm turning in on itself, sweeping over the buried life: eyes wide, alive.

But, here's the important thing: you don't rebuild with the same pieces—you remove the heavy parts, let them fall away. Layer by layer. Belief by belief:

all the unkind words you've learned and held onto; (even when they fell from the mouth of someone carrying too much pain). The second language of limitation, and guilt, and shame, you've taught yourself to believe, (because it's easier to believe). The illusion that you're not quite good enough as you are, that you're separate, that it's you against the world, that life will never get better, that this is all there is. Everything. Everything dimming your light, breathing through your cells like a tortured, second self, has to be free. Because, underneath all that chaos and complexity, you are as fresh, and alive, as a flower in the rain.

And that's where you start from, because that's where you bloom from.

April Green

the intention to grow
instantly creates a space
for your body to step into.

but, unless you let go of
everything weighing you down,
that space dissolves into air

like a broken promise.

April Green

The art of honesty

I think that when you're entirely honest with yourself, a door opens within, and the light unfolds, and everything painful flies away.

April Green

The wild

I live with a constant hunger for the wild—and it's always just a barefooted step away; like a little tug of gravity, a quiet possibility, that, while the Earth is moving and turning, maybe I could too.

Because I want to be, again, that girl who stood up to the ocean, arms open and fearless; flesh dripping with courage and an inexplicable touch of being free. And I mean free, like the blue air of eternity, like summer all the time, like daisies and dusk, salt and dirt free. Like waking up with sunshine in my mouth and birdsong in my hair, tangled and trembling with the weight of rebellion.

And all that light through my bones; white as a feather.

April Green

Wildflowers and rain

Something about the thought of starting over: that tiny glimmer of light, a breath reaching out to me, whispering my worth, helped me see that all I had to do was give myself permission to take one step in a new direction, just one step towards a new life.

And so, I pressed the scent of fearlessness, of wildflowers and rain, of running and stumbling and falling towards a life ahead of me, into my wrists like a mark of anticipation.

I started to bring back to life that which was once as real and alive as my beating heart.

April Green

the taste of another chance,
rising like a promise at the back of your throat,
should give you the courage to look more closely
at all the things that are causing you pain.

we all deserve another chance:
not a second chance—another chance.

(the earth gives us as many chances as we need)

April Green

The build-up of pain

I think pain builds up in our lives when we take small problems, that we know we can deal with, and we make them bigger ourselves to try and feel more in control. But, all we end up doing is developing a habit of redirecting our focus away from that which scares us the most: the root cause of our pain.

But, in my experience, the only way to feel everything (fully) and be free, is to delve into the part of yourself that you don't want to face. *Reach into the truth of who you really are,* because hiding who you are from yourself invites destruction into your life. But, when you're brave enough to get right down to the root cause of your pain, you start the process of loosening it, unravelling it, freeing it from the core. You unfold the destruction before it folds in on you. You get to take control over *all* of the pain in your life, because all of the pain in your life comes from the root.

And, when you decide to face your truth, then it's okay if you don't feel ready to show people who you really are; you have to show yourself first. It takes time. Live with your authentic self, as you are—vulnerable, raw, beautiful. Learn about yourself, breathe your own air for a while, be gentle.

The pain will eventually fly from your body.

April Green

An altered state

I spent too many years suppressing my emotions; never allowing myself to truly *feel* them. I was too terrified of the pain— the love, the loss, the grief, the wars heaped against my bones, that I never gave myself the chance to experience them all completely; I never gave myself the chance to become altered by them. I labelled each emotion, I just never allowed myself to experience the way in which each emotion moved me.

It wasn't until my healing process, that I learned that the fear of feeling an emotion is much more terrifying than the actual experience of feeling that emotion. Because, once you release a suppressed emotion, you free up so much space inside you that you actually feel lighter. And it's not about misplacing the emotion or projecting it onto someone else. It's about detaching yourself from it, releasing it; viewing it as a completely new emotion without any meaning or memory behind it.

Emotions need to be released, not held onto. Where would a river go if it were able to hold back its flow? It would turn in on itself. It would implode, spill out, destroy everything around it.

Don't hold back on an emotion; don't leave it inside you for later because you're too afraid to deal with it now. To ignore the pain is to disown the root. To

April Green

avoid it, to store it away, to hide it from yourself, is just another way of carrying it with you; just another way of giving it power. It's as if to say: 'my body is yours, rest here, weigh it down with all I can't face, do what you will to it.'

But, your body is not an enemy, it is not a battleground—it is your home.

April Green

'i'm going to let go,' i whispered to the air.'

'because, i understand now how the wildflowers grow.'

Becoming a wildflower

Wildflowers grow wherever the wind takes them; wherever the wind chooses to lay them down, they grow.

They don't look at their environment or the circumstances that brought them to where they are. They don't look at who is next to them, in front of them, or behind them.

They turn their faces to the light; and they grow.

April Green

whatever you do...

do it with astonishing bravery

and strength

April Green

Returning

The memory comes back to me now, almost close enough to touch: the dense purple dusk, a bruise pressed into the air. Perhaps, the stain of my thoughts leaving me, or returning to me, I didn't know, but it felt like forever in a moment; and it changed every moment forever.

Surrendering. Letting go. Giving (what felt like) my last breath to a space between body and air. The entire weight of despair pulled from under bones; crushed between earth and wood and cotton and skin, where every movement moved something else, held palms up: flowers drinking the last drop of light.

And there was light. I felt it breaking inside me: fragments of all the beautiful faith I once had.

Returning.

April Green

Acceptance

Acceptance creates a tremendous altering: a shift in the stars, a different kind of air through your lungs. Because, when you let something go, it is *you* who becomes free.

It is you who allows the walls to come down. It is you who unfolds the pain and sets it free. And it is you who creates a space for everything new to come towards you, freely.

Acceptance is your true self creating a tiny miracle.

April Green

Hold on

When I let go, I remember holding onto something tighter than I've ever held before:

to the vision I had for myself. To the dream lying beside me like a burning, breathing star.

And I think that's how it happens: once your dream starts tugging at your soul, you learn how to very quietly, and very softly, loosen your grip on anything getting in the way of that dream.

April Green

hold tight to your

dream

not to the thing
holding you back from
reaching that dream.

April Green

The taste of faith

I woke to the taste of faith and sunlight: a bluebird inside my heart, the sound of a different song. And like the shedding of a second skin, I was lighter, unburdened. The pain had gone; it had nothing to hold onto anymore. It was as though I had been emptied and filled in the space of a whispered prayer, a newly granted wish.

What I learned about honesty then. What I learned about the truth, spoken from my mouth, through the air, through the mountains I'd been trying to move.

I think the Earth has ways of teaching you that it will only move with you, not for you.

And when you take the first step; when you dance with the wind, and the stars, each step becomes lighter because each step is a mark of faith; and faith is opening your heart like a lotus flower and allowing the pain to be free.

April Green

even now, all i can think is this:

'how light and simple everything becomes when you have a dream to reach and the earth's hand holding yours when you need it the most.'

Cycles

It's beautiful really: the way we break ourselves, only to hurt, and heal, and learn, and breathe—until the moon falls down and we rise in new bones.

April Green

some people's presence renews you:

it reminds you that
you have to open your hands
to hold new life.

April Green

Two worlds

It's impossible to breathe new air when you're living between two worlds: one half desperately clinging to what you know, the other half helplessly begging you to leave it all behind. It's an unbalanced and chaotic place to even try and build a life upon.

But when I found myself living like that for many years, I couldn't see any other options; I didn't feel worthy of living any other way. The past always appeared in front of me; lingering, circling, one step ahead. I truly believed that it defined me; that *I* was my past, and that everyone else could see what I could see.

I didn't understand that you can stop looking at the past whenever you decide to; even when it's showing up behind you, in front of you, or inside you. You can stop looking. You can choose to start again, *wherever you are, whoever you are, whatever you have done.*

Stop judging yourself—no-one sees your past; they see *you*, as you are.

Free yourself from the past by jumping through the air, eyes closed, hands ready to build something new on the other side.

April Green

'what does it feel like to be free?' she asked.

'the cage door isn't locked,' i said. 'see how it feels…

fly.'

April Green

I've been thinking

I've been thinking about how some of us end up in the grip of something so painful yet so normal (for us) that the fear of leaving it becomes more painful than anything else. And I think it's because we become so lost that we end up in a place we can't describe, or even put into words—it's like a place of unbelonging; as though our hearts creep slowly from our ribs, leaving the bones of us spinning in orbit with a galaxy of strangers.

And I've been trying to work out why it surfaces inside of us in the first place: I think it's when we (unconsciously) lose the connection to our true nature—love. And I think we lose the connection because we don't feel it within ourselves, we don't recognise it, we don't know it's inside us. We forget.

I'm not saying that love isn't given to us; I'm saying that *when* love is given, it doesn't connect, it bounces off us. And I think that during some time, some trauma, some slow, insidious happening, we turned away from the very nature of love; we turned away from ourselves.

What I'm trying to say, is that the way we behave to compensate for feeling like we don't belong will keep

April Green

showing up in our lives until we understand why the feeling visited us in the first place. It will keep showing up until we start re-connecting with ourselves, with our true nature, with love.

Because, I think it's very sad to live, for many years, in a way that feels like home to our minds, to what we tell ourselves, to what we hide from ourselves, but is desperately destructive to our souls.

April Green

never underestimate
the strength it takes
to let feelings
fall from your mouth
like tears.

a note on depression:

try and find a way to make every inhale taste
beautiful again.

(the sun will eventually find its way back to you)

Love.
breathe.

you belong here.

Lessons

I think there is one thing more important than forgiving yourself for the past, and that's learning to stop carrying it into the future with you.

April Green

The greatest freedom

I have learned, (I am still learning), that when your time is spent trying to work out why something has happened, why something has gone wrong, why a door has closed, then all the goodness and clarity that's available to you becomes concealed inside a cloud of blinding fog.

But, if you could just see the breakthrough that comes from letting go of heavy thoughts and feelings, (and I promise it comes as clearly as though you were seeing the same sunset at the same time each day), then you wouldn't hesitate in opening your hands to a breath of new air.

The greatest freedom you can achieve is in accepting that some things in life are out of your control; but the choice to transform the space you are left with is yours. *You're in control of that choice.*

April Green

The spirit of you

When you let go of what's holding you back; when you take a leap of faith, you don't leave your spirit behind.

Your spirit, the very essence of who you are and who you are becoming, is the very thing that carries you.

April Green

Heartbreak

Heartbreak can empty the ocean. It can pull the life from your bones and move it to another world. It can make you forget that your heart was ever once unbroken, forget that love was ever there at all. But it was there; and it emanated from you, it awakened from you.

Energy, (love), cannot be planted inside you, it can only be expanded. If you have been loved, know that *you* were producing that love. *Whatever you see in someone else is a recognition of what you already have within yourself.*

If ever it feels like your heart is breaking, it's because you have allowed pain to blend into its beat. But the love is still there; and you can learn how to untangle it from the pain, as though you're sifting rose dust from earth, and fold it back into your body. Because, it's yours.

It will always be yours.

April Green

Love notes

The energy of love is what we were born with, and it never leaves us. Do you understand? It never leaves us. We leave love: we turn away from it each time we go looking for it. We see it in other people, and we want it for ourselves, completely unaware that in doing so, we're turning the energy of love into the energy of ingratitude, jealousy, and disenchantment—the kind of emotions that send a message into the ether of: 'I don't want love.'

Please do not spend any more days chasing that which is already inside you—chase the days when love was your default setting: the sun in your bones, the moon beneath your skin.

April Green

We ask people to stay

I think we ask people to stay because we're scared they'll take pieces of us away with them if they leave.

But nothing that comes from within us ever really leaves: it stays in our bones like the gold in a leaf. It's in memory. It is written.

April Green

Trust the stars

It's hard to understand why some things are put on your path when there's no apparent reason, or why some things are taken as swiftly as the brushing away of falling tears. But, if you trust that there *is* a reason as much as you trust in your very next breath, then you get to take control.

The stars are always aligning for you: they don't need your help, they just need you to believe in them.

April Green

in silence,
faith moves you forward—

it takes you from spaces
no longer for you.

it walks you to spaces that are.

April Green

The paradox of letting go

I think some of us are afraid of being ourselves. And I think some of us are afraid of losing the identities we've built up over the years, so we sit somewhere in the middle; never really getting to know exactly who we are. But, if there's one thing I've learned, it's that you *have* to lose the mask of who you think people want you to be if you want to grow into the person you deserve to be. I guess it's like the chipping away of marble: only when it's removed does the beauty of the art reveal itself; raw, natural, and exquisitely real.

You can't take any part of your old self into your new world; it gets in the way of who you really want to be.

Letting go shows that you have a strong sense of knowing who you are, and where you're going. It's about accepting that you can't control the fluidity of life; it's about freeing yourself from the things you are hiding behind.

Letting go gives you endless space to grow.

April Green

sometimes,
(before you even know you need it)
your heart has already
given you the
answer.

April Green

Silent knowing

Walking away from someone takes courage. But if you know in your heart that a person is diminishing your light, causing you to shrink, making you feel discomfort, pulling you out of alignment, then letting that person go sends a strong message to yourself that you are not willing to settle.

Listen to every internal message because your heart is helping you raise your self-worth.

Never doubt the decisions you make based on the way your heart is feeling. Learning to trust a message that comes through to you from your own body, your silent knowing, is the most honourable thing you can do for yourself.

April Green

Wisdom from within

I used to ignore intuition if it was telling me something I didn't want to believe. But, only once I'd gone around and around in a never-ending circle of pleasing and denying and shrinking and trying... to make things right, did I understand that intuition is never wrong.

The signs you ignore in the first place are the reasons you make your next big move.

April Green

Lost love

I think the saddest thing of all is that when we find something beautifully loving in a person, we don't always realise that it's a reflection of ourselves; and instead, we feel unworthy of it and we push it away.

April Green

true connections happen
only when each person is connected
deeply to themselves.

How it happens

Sometimes, you don't always realise you've let go until you wake up one day completely free of the attachment—as though it's fallen from your body like moonlight from a dawn sky.

That's how easily it happens.

Once you start noticing all the beautiful things you're already living with, you stop thinking about the things you once thought you couldn't live without.

April Green

Promise yourself

Promise that you will never settle when the days get tough, and you think you're not enough. Then, promise yourself that you will keep that promise. Because, everything tastes like love when you're lonely, and your intuitive sense, the heart within the heart, gets forced into the cold. The value you place upon yourself, (your worth), gets forgotten about, trampled to the ground. And by the time you need to call upon it, you're already feeling worthless: you have to start healing all over again.

Know that loneliness diminishes when you understand what drives you into feeling more connected to life—whether that's the Earth beneath your feet, saltwater against your skin, or the pen between your fingers.

Fully connecting with something your soul is drawing you towards helps you connect deeply to yourself. And deeply connecting to yourself helps you connect fully with everything else. It's like an exchange:

when you bloom for yourself, your petals touch everything around you.

April Green

do not chase love
or perfection
or attention
or validation.

do not chase any of these things.

chase the call of the wild
the song in your heart
the ocean in your bones.

chase the freedom
to roam
and dream
and fall
in time with the setting sun.

April Green

Find a blessing in the pain

Anger blinds you; it blocks the bigger plan from ever unfolding. If you want to move on from a person, you can't have any negative feelings towards that person. Do not become angry or bitter. Do not try and find any sense behind it; (some things are beyond understanding) otherwise they will stay alive in front of your eyes.

Instead, learn how to calm and quieten the mind by focusing on the person you are becoming. Don't look for the thought that is causing you pain, look for the thought that *isn't* causing you pain. Once you can do this, you will immediately, and very naturally, turn away from the pain (you can't focus on two things at once).

Blessings come out of pain; but you will only see them once you allow the pain to become free.

New doors are always opening for you, but you will only see them once you close your eyes to hurt and anger. And, when the stillness in your mind settles like sleep, doors will open within you too. Something you once desired, something you've been putting off doing, will rise within you like a blood red moon.

Pain, betrayal, injustice, always lead you back to yourself—*learn how to stay there.*

April Green

- 49 -

Something else decides

Life doesn't always seem fair. Things that you think are for you, sometimes go past you: people change, people leave, life moves on. It sometimes feels as though your own life is completely out of your hands. And, it is—it's in the hands of something much bigger than you, something working only for your good.

Please, have faith. For faith is everything: it is trusting. It is the letting-in that comes from letting go. It is new air, fresh perspective, looking ahead. It is not worrying about 'if it will,' or 'how it will,' just knowing that it will.

April Green

Your worth

Letting go becomes easier, more natural, more organic, once you learn how to put a higher value on yourself. Because, when you cherish your heart, you start investing more time and energy into your physical and emotional health, and something shifts: you stop re-visiting the pain; you start looking towards the person you are becoming.

Your worth leads the way.

April Green

don't lose sight of everything good
that's coming towards you because
you're too busy clinging to something
that doesn't serve you.

Let go of letting go

Don't fool yourself into thinking you have let go just because you have told yourself you have. Don't become lost in the chaotic space between holding on and letting go. Because, whether you're holding back the thing you don't want in your life or clinging to the thing you want but can't have; your hands are tied— bound to one thing instead of free to touch everything beautiful floating your way.

When you let go of thinking about letting go, you will instantly clear a space for happiness, love, creativity, and freedom to get through. You will start enjoying each moment as it comes, rather than missing each moment because your thoughts are still clinging to what you *think* will make you happy.

When you can grasp this, you are on the way to letting go.

April Green

whatever i imagine comes to me
in a way i never imagined.

that's how it works.

that's what happens when you let go of
all control and simply allow the energy to
decide.

April Green

Let love in

Letting go is a feeling; it's a release of all the resistance you have placed between yourself and the very thing in which you are trying so hard to let go.

Know that the emotions you're feeling: anger, sadness, loneliness, hurt, are creating within you an unwillingness to accept the situation for what it is. And while you're carrying these emotions around with you; you're carrying the situation around with you too. Strong emotions that don't feel good inside your body create a storm of negative energy which does not allow the situation, person, or thing to pass through.

And I know, from my heart to yours, that you think it will hurt too much to let go, (fear is the most potent form of resistance), but please believe me when I tell you that it hurts more to hold on.

Love yourself. Love other people (without any attachment to an outcome), accept things as they are, be grateful for the lessons.

Love, acceptance and gratitude, are the emotions that will free you, for these are the emotions that create miracles. I promise.

April Green

when you let go—

i hope you look back and see that
you were holding onto nothing
but pain.

April Green

Letting it be

Letting it go feels easier when you translate it to: 'letting it *be*, exactly as it is.'

Don't fight with energy: bravery is when you allow yourself to feel the hurt (and the sadness), while accepting that you can't change it. The energy you're using to hold on or to hold back, can instead be used to move forward at the same pace as life.

Let whatever comes come. It takes courage and practice, but it softens you. The world holding you up will no longer feel like it's crumbling around you; it will feel like it's moving through you.

Even the wild air.

April Green

when i was rebuilding myself:

i collected all the broken flowers
and turned them into something
very beautiful.

April Green

the bravery of wearing

a new life . . .

of letting go

April Green

You

Before you let go, remember:

Everything about you is important: the little things, the marks on you, the secrets you fold behind your heart, the notes you write yourself and tuck inside your favourite book, the music you love, the dreams you have, the words you speak, the stories you tell. And, all that pain you hold between your ribs like an injured bird you're not yet ready to set free—
everything.

Everything about you is important because it's all of you. It's who you are. Understand this. Don't change anything for anyone just because you're afraid of their perception of you. Become the brightest light and let them adjust to you for a change. Keep hold of all that you can until you decide if any of it is holding you back. And then you have the choice to let it go... when *you* are ready.

April Green

and

'do you still break? 'she asked.

'sometimes,' i said. 'but it's softer now;
it doesn't hurt as much.'

April Green

unlearning

the things i was taught
and
learning about myself
instead.

Lost and found

And I would tell anyone to get so lost in the journey
of finding themselves, that they never want to ever
go back.

April Green

The journey of self-love

Somewhere far back in my life, in some undefinable way, I believed I wasn't good enough; so I started pleasing people, agreeing with people, folding my voice away like an old t-shirt that no longer fits. When my light started to dim, I merely grew more accustomed to the dark; gathering it into my arms like a make-believe friend, a silent comfort. Some nights, I valued myself so little, I swear even the stars started moving further away from me. And isn't that the most terrifying thing about not feeling good enough? You repel everything good and beautiful away from you until you feel smaller, and lonelier, and more isolated than ever before.

But, each morning the flowers would curl around my ribs again. Buds like fists would stretch and open, like a hundred dreams unfolding. The scent of sweetness, of soft mercy, would hit the back of my throat like an answer, and I would think:

'If only I could find the piece that connects me to something more, then maybe I could start believing in more. Maybe I could start believing that the empty spaces I've been digging haven't been for me after all, but for the seeds of my dreams to fill.'

And that's how it works; that's how it begins—the journey of self-love: *believing* you are enough.

April Green

and each time you declare your self-worth—

to yourself
to the space between the air
to the earth beneath your bones
to the oceans and mountains and rivers and sky;

the stars move closer to earth.

April Green

Finding your way back

I understand how easy it is to step away from the energy of love, how easy it is to fall out of alignment with the source of life. How do you join the dance when you've slipped so far away that it feels like everything's spinning out of reach?

The first thing you must do is turn around, change direction, shift your perspective. Understand that a miracle can only occur with a shift in thought, an awareness, a glimpse of colour: dappled sunlight catching your eye.

Because, there *is* light inside the darkness; that's how you found your way in there. You just have to turn around first, in order to find your way back out.

April Green

i can't heal you—but i can give you the space here

and here

and here
and here

and here

and here   and here

and here

to remind you that healing lives inside you.

(begin. by remembering)

April Green

your breath has prayer in it.

and flowers, and rain, and salt
from the ocean's shifting tide.

> i never think about the woman i was
> yesterday—i have felt earth break beneath
> my knees with the soft fall of surrender.

i know that change is possible.

April Green

The thing about healing

The thing about healing is that it's introspective: you learn how to do it by yourself from within yourself, and for yourself.

Healing should be treated as precious as air: both keep you alive.

April Green

we heal others

when we heal

ourselves

April Green

Face your fears instead of judging others

We see in others what we are in ourselves; and others see in us what they are in themselves.

When I am out of balance with myself, I sometimes see the worst in a person and, deep down, I know it's because I'm seeing a part of myself that I've rejected and forced into the shadows. I'm seeing a wound I've not yet faced, a grief I've not yet breathed, a pain I've hidden beneath bones. I'm seeing everything that I can't bring myself to face, projected onto another person.

When we can't face our own fears, we tend to judge others to try and make ourselves feel better. But, I've learned that it's easier to take these moments of discomfort and use them to become more self-aware; to notice your patterns and behaviours. For these moments are gifts: they're teaching you that, unless you embrace that which you've pushed into the shadows, it will invariably spill out in some way or another. It will keep returning in a different disguise until you let it teach you an important lesson, (for your growth).

If ever you feel yourself judging others, stop and ask yourself: 'what is the real problem here? What are

April Green

you afraid of?' Feel it, speak it out of yourself and you will see that you are never really upset for the reason you think you are.

a softness exists within you.

it is grace. it is eternal grace.

and i think it's important to
always try and breathe from this place.

April Green

Balance

Finding balance is something I have to work on relentlessly; and it's tough when you're an all or nothing person like me. Whenever I feel any kind of emotion, my default setting is at the extreme end of the spectrum: a wave crashing against me, or a wave pulling the life from my bones. Balance for me is keeping myself grounded inside the highs and lows of life.

Like many of us, I have suffered great loss, bereavement, shock, and trauma, all in a very short space of time. The physical scars from a serious illness remain with me today. And while I'm reminded of them each time I dress and undress, I'm also reminded how my body kept me alive; accepted every invasive treatment thrown at her, and still knitted herself back together like a beautiful, patchwork quilt. I look at things differently, I see the textures behind everything, the pain behind the smiles, the scars as jewels; as messengers sent to heal the greater parts of us.

It's okay to take your time achieving balance: it's *your* balance; your life, your journey. You may have

April Green

to unlearn the things you thought you knew. You may have to start choosing to live life more on your terms: *stop doing what everyone else is doing.*

You will definitely have to say 'no' more often.

But, more than all of this—make sure you start the journey of healing by clearing the energy of past trauma so that you don't transfer it into every space the sun is leading you towards. *You are not responsible for your past trauma, but only you can decide whether to keep allowing it to live with you.*

Your awareness of aiming for balance is, in itself, helping you become balanced.

April Green

i have a secret:

it takes time to learn
the language of
self-love.

April Green

Everything passes

I know myself well enough to notice when my energy is heading towards a dark corner. Warning signs appear as flashbacks from memories stored in a chamber labelled 'do not enter,' and they play over and over like the beat of a heart. I know I'm the only one who can change the channel; (nothing is pulling these flashbacks towards me except my own energy), but when you're crouched in a corner like a leaf brought in by the wind, you can't reach the switch. Your eyes are burning everything in sight. You can't see reality. You can't see the living. You can only see the ashes of the past.

So, the one thing I've taught myself to do is to reach for the opposite to how I'm feeling: somehow, inch by inch, breath by breath, I try to find some kind of emotional relief, some kind of improved way of thinking; the smallest, tiniest, better feeling thought. And this is usually the only spark I need to get me moving out of such a dark place.

Know yourself, stay close to yourself, don't wander. Everything passes when you breathe with the energy of life.

April Green

and through every

part of the storm

she understood

the importance

of grace

Self-reflection

Self-reflection is something I do as regularly as I check the time. What am I thinking about, or in other words, what am I giving my energy to? When you make time for self-reflection, you are given back the time you would otherwise have spent with dark matter.

Self-reflection helps me understand what exactly causes negative energy to sweep over my bones like a breeze through an open window. I want to understand because I'm the one who's responsible for my wellbeing—I owe it to my heart to find out exactly what triggers these dark periods.

I know they happen when I move away from myself too much. When I read too much news, when I don't spend enough time alone. *The warning signs are always there: you just have to learn how to listen to them more closely.* I try to be kind to myself, first and foremost. I walk, write, create, eat well, and try to keep my life as simple as I can. I've said this before, but there is gold to be found in the little things.

By practicing meditation, grounding, and self-awareness, clarity appears and reminds me that I've

April Green

been there before, I got through it before.

Everything passes as long as you give everything the space to pass through.

Own your life

And if you are happy with what you have; with what you have achieved; with everything that brings you joy, and relief, and gratitude—don't ever allow those feelings to be tainted by someone who isn't happy with what they have.

If anyone questions your choices, it's only because your choices aren't right for *them*.

Never forget this: you're not making your choices for them—you're making them for yourself.

April Green

note to self:

i am not defined
by what other people
think about me.

my opinion of myself
is what matters.

(anyone else's opinion of me belongs to them)

April Green

Stay true to you

Embrace the truth of who you are—honestly and passionately. Don't become a version of the person you think other people want you to be. Because, when you aren't being yourself, you attract people who aren't like yourself; and they will pull you along a path that isn't meant for you. But, when you allow all that magic, authentic, raw energy to pour from your soul like sweet honey, you attract everything that belongs to you.

April Green

The most important things are the things you
learn yourself

I fit into myself more comfortably when I'm alone.

I work better when I'm doing something from the
soul.

I let things go much quicker because when they
cling to me it hurts.

Just because I have healed from everything holding
me back, doesn't mean I still can't break. It's softer.

Forgiving myself for a thing usually stops me from
re-living that thing.

I'm gentler on my past: self-compassion sits with me
more often than self-pity does.

I feel too much, and that's okay. It's a gift, not a
curse.

I'm still learning the language of self-love.

I will always be still learning the language of self-
love.

Some days, I'm all of the things I'm fighting against
being.

April Green

The important things I want you to know

It's very easy to ruin something good: life is as fragile as air.

Do not chase after that which has already left. Love and nurture the things you want to stay; and, if they eventually leave, you will still be fuller than before.

Self-punishment is self-harm, is beating your bones from the inside then expecting yourself to get up and walk further next time. Stay soft with yourself; practice self-compassion.

Things really do flow into your life for a reason: learn, explore, and enjoy the reasons. If you try to control the force of nature, you will only be left behind.

Don't step into anyone else's state of mind; don't allow yourself to be drawn towards energy that isn't created by you.

Do everything with purpose. *Your* life matters.

Every broken piece doesn't need to be collected or analysed. Some things need to stay lost; because they don't belong to you anymore, (and they probably never did).

April Green

Everything falls into place

Sometimes, I look back and realise that the thing I thought was breaking me was actually growing me. It just didn't feel like that at the time—it felt like the world had ended in the space of a thousand tiny earthquakes and the taste of falling rain.

April Green

learning to love yourself
won't always be easy.

there will be times
when you won't feel
good enough.

you will feel alone.
you will question
why you're here; still,
with all this darkness clinging
to your wrists
like the scent of winter rain.

but then, dawn will appear:

and oh, all that light.

April Green

A place beyond the stars

It's the only place where I can have an honest conversation with myself; the only place where the truth of who I am reveals itself like a fresh memory.

Solitude—my refuge from life—the only place that brings me back to life.

April Green

healing is:

allowing flowers to grow
in all the places sadness has touched
inside you.

The relationship you have with yourself

Everything that happens to you in life always comes back to the relationship you have with yourself. Every emotion, every feeling, every trigger fuelling those feelings, arises from the connection you have with yourself. So, in order to evolve into a stronger person, you first have to start deepening the relationship you have with yourself. And if you're open to befriending and accepting all of yourself, (instead of rejecting some parts), then you are already deepening that relationship.

It's about bringing into your awareness all the things you've pushed into the shadows—all the parts you've rejected—the wounds you're not prepared to face, the pain you've buried, the traits you dislike.

Learn how to express them. Feel them. Put the energy of them into something creative.

Then, accept them for what they are: part of you. Because, knowing yourself, shadow and light, gets the balance back into the construction of who you are, which helps develop the relationship you have with yourself. You see, there are a multitude of versions of you: old, new, changing, fractured,

April Green

broken, unbroken, evolving. We're like works of art: unfinished, always in progress.

Self-awareness is about finding something new each time you visit yourself. It's a lush and beautiful flux, a wild world, a Universe, and it's all you really have... the relationship with yourself. All other relationships grow from that one; they join at each heart, connect with each beat. And they only happen organically, naturally, when you have a deep connection with yourself, (at that very moment), and when you are open and honest with yourself, (at that very moment). Connections are more like a remembering: a time when you were deeply connected to life. And, once you realise that you are always in a state of becoming, life becomes one beautiful, lush adventure.

April Green

and if you ever have one of those days
when you feel like you're not enough,
just become yourself—more passionately,
more lovingly, and more intensely than
ever before.

April Green

Honour the past

It's easy to push the dark periods away, to try and remove them from your story, but remember: if you are everything minus your past then you are nothing.

The dark patches of the past make up the fabric of who you are now. Accept them, be tender with them, forgive them.

Look back at your past as a way of honouring just how far you've come.

April Green

i don't think
there should be any shame
in the soft revolution
that starts inside your heart
the minute you decide
to have a better relationship
with yourself.

April Green

You still shine

And if some days all you can do is exist, like the fading winter sun, please remember that you still shine—maybe not as brightly as a day when there are no clouds in the sky—but you still shine.

Give yourself these days to practice self-compassion, fill your heart with soft words, rest, breathe, be still.

Allow the act of patience to become the sunlight for you.

April Green

and
her small,
flowered heart
just kept
blooming.

don't be afraid to speak it,
(the thing that's important to you)

and if you can't speak it,
then say it in some form of art.

because, if it's important to you
then it must be expressed.

storing everything up into silence
is the kind of habit that fills you with nothing
but pain.

April Green

that freedom you achieve
when you only focus on what matters most
to you—

stay unapologetic about that freedom.

April Green

and even when everything

looks dark to your eyes —

i still see you shine

Become the moon

If the fear of not being accepted, or good enough, makes you shrink and hide—like a whisper stitched into shadow—then you must become the moon:

> you must rise and become so full of self-belief that even the stars won't know what to do with themselves.

April Green

Love notes:

When you start healing the part of yourself that you think is lacking something; you will soon see that all it is lacking is your own love and acceptance.

healing is a process.

if you love yourself throughout the process,
then you are healing.

don't be hard on yourself.

stay gentle.

and
if ever you feel yourself breaking—
you can take that feeling and
turn it into gold.

April Green

It is your life

Not everyone will understand who you are, but that doesn't mean you have to explain who you are. Preserve your 'self.' Your footprint is unique: there is no-one else like you.

Your life should be a continuous expression of who you are—a sacred season, a re-invention, a movement.

It should not be an explanation or an apology.

It is your life. Create whatever you want from it.

April Green

whoever you are—be that.

for you are too breathtakingly unique to ever hide
yourself from the world.

April Green

Find what matters

For some, transformation happens very quickly. For others, it's a slower process: deep questions require deeper, wider reflection in order for the answers to surface. *Quick fixes are never the solution—they only lead you further into the fog.*

The process of transformation involves looking at your entire life, your beliefs, your patterns of thought, your choices, your habits, your mistakes— because these are the things that have brought you to the place you want to move away from. Look at them closely, hold them, unravel them, and you will very quickly notice that so many of them are programmed responses that you're repeating without even thinking.

The intention to change leads you to an awareness of what you need to change.

For me, it was the belief that I wasn't good enough; that the past was defining me, that I couldn't move on. *I was looking at my future through the eyes of my past.*

The next stage of transformation is to take responsibility for these (false) beliefs. Spread forgiveness over them, the way the sun spreads gold

April Green

over a wild sea.   And if you have to leave some big things behind, like a job or a relationship, then know that these are only drops in the ocean compared to the depth of your whole life. Transformation is about building a space in your life where *you* can be happy; a space where *you* can grow.

Carve it out (for yourself) with your own hands, nobody else's. Don't invite anything into your space if you think it's going to hold you back.

Listen to your heart: allow only those things that matter most to you into your space.

Forgive yourself

You are so much more than your past, so much greater than your mistakes. It is only you who re-lives them in your mind time and time again. And, it is only you who can press the off switch.

Don't become a prisoner to a time when you simply didn't know any better; when you were confused and thought that the very moment you were living was your whole life, and it would define your whole life. It didn't. It was simply a moment leading to a thousand moments, then a thousand more.

Remember this: there are things in life that must happen to you in order for you to learn. And, the truth is, you will learn (and let go) in your own time. You will make terrible mistakes. You will choose certain loves unwisely. You will ignore your heart more times than you will admit to. You will stay inside the energy of comfort. You will turn your whole life upside down a hundred times over. And, you will do it always from the side of fear—the fear of being left behind, of losing yourself in a storm, of not being enough, of being too much, of silence, and language, and breathing—the fear of living.

And, when you've had enough of pushing and

April Green

bending an unchanging law, you will learn to forgive yourself. You will learn to embrace yourself.

You can't right the wrongs, but if you keep reacting based on the past, you will continue in the same pattern. It is only through awareness, and honesty that you learn to stop repeating the same mistakes. You learn how to transcend them, meaning: you break the spiral of repeating old behaviours.

You close the chapter with the breeze of your wings.

April Green

When a storm passes through

Just before your mind takes flight, and your body parts separate like paper scattering through the air; and the light goes, and the legs un-hold you, and things start fading away: there's a space. Just before that violent moment, there's a space, a three second space where, if you say the words: 'I'm safe here, this is a safe place, my feet are resting on something solid and my heart's where it belongs,' something invisible holds you, I swear.

And the secret is *believing* in that something. I promise that's why it works.

April Green

resilience:

you fall
and
you rise
within the same
heartbeat.

April Green

it's not the fall that matters.

it's what you do afterwards;
it's how you pick yourself back up.

the fear of being who you truly are
is the biggest cause of unhappiness,
the longest breath of confusion.
and, the truth is…
easier to accept when you realise
you're the only one who thinks about it.
meaning:
i'm still figuring things out.
i'm still learning about myself.
i'm a bird whose wings were once broken;
i'm remembering who i am.
and, more importantly: i accept that i can still be,
very slowly, or very suddenly, pulled
towards something else.
the difference between catching a falling feather,
or watching it fall to the ground:
nothing is fixed. it's fluid, it's moving.

that's what makes it all so beautiful.

April Green

I believe

I believe in a power much stronger than us, and I believe it resides within us—a spark connecting us to the whole of the cosmos— the stars, the Earth, the ocean, each other. I believe that when we set an intention, (good or bad), it's recorded by the ether and returned to us through the voices of others, through symbols, and dreams, and signs. Because all of these things share the same spark, they communicate in a silent language, hear everything, miss nothing.

Even the way we speak to ourselves, (about ourselves, and other people) is returned to us in some form or another; which is why I believe in goodness:

I think if you are good to yourself, you will naturally be good to others. And then goodness will fall into your hands as though everything beautiful you've ever held is yours to hold again.

April Green

and

i hope you feel

my prayers

(even when i don't speak them)

Destination addiction

You think you want something. But it's only the feeling you think it will give you that you want. You want more of something because you think it will make you feel better. You want to be somewhere in the future because you think happiness lives there. You want to be in someone's arms because you think love will pass from their bones to yours.

But I need you to see that all you're really doing is chasing moments (that haven't even surfaced), in the hope they will lead you somewhere else. You're attached to the false belief that everything in the future tastes better than everything in the present moment. It's a belief that will keep you exactly where you are, and you will feel nothing but empty.

Instead, take the energy you're using to chase all of these illusions, and pull it back from the air—direct it towards something happening in the *now*. Know that you can train your mind to become less attached to needing to find external sources of happiness, by focusing it on something happening in the *now.*

Each time you want more, use that energy to *do* more: act upon it. Energetic desire only works for

April Green

you in the now. It creates a space right next to you in the now. If you focus on wanting something better, that space will simply dissolve into dust.

learning to be present
is the closest thing to perfection you can get.
because, the energy in that place is like
Gods own breath.

Reflecting the cosmos

'Keep me here forever,' she said, 'on this wild island of flowers, and dreams, and waves that taste like everyone I've ever loved returning.'

And I watch her for a second, radiating her light beneath the arched back of the moon, and I think:

'We are human stars: we carry eternity within us, always.'

April Green

Pray the right way

Have you ever noticed that as soon as you stop putting all of your energy into wanting something, you receive it, or something equivalent, or better? It's because you dropped the thought of it; you turned away from it, *you focused on something else.*

Desperately wanting something creates a magnet of resistance that holds it away from you because, wanting something is telling the Universe that you think you're lacking something. And when you think you're lacking something, it becomes a feeling which is expressed as ingratitude. It's as though your energy changes to a heavy, metal fog that creates a barrier between you and the air.

You have to shift it. Stop praying (in lack) for things you don't have and start praying (in gratitude) for things you already have. It's a simple shift, and it creates a miracle.

April Green

Poetry in motion

Notice the times when you are reminded about all that is beautiful about being human—the times when you are broken open, and emptied, and filled in a single heartbeat.

Life is a moving poem.

April Green

A mark of happiness

Too often, we talk about our pain and our scars—the marks of the past that stay with us like indelible bruises under our skin.   But, what about the incredibly happy moments: what mark do they leave upon us and why don't we wear them more often?

Lately, I've started recording moments as I see them, because I want to remember everything. I want to learn from the pleasure, not just from the pain.

April Green

Dependence

Please kill the part of you that believes that your happiness is dependent on another person or another thing, that your dreams won't come true, that you will never be enough, that you don't deserve love.

There is a power deep inside you that can rise above all of these false beliefs. Find it. Nurture it.

April Green

Your power

Start summoning enough bravery to believe in yourself for a change. *Nothing is untrue if you want it to be true.*

You become weak when you depend on things outside of yourself to help you: your power is within you. When you look for it outside, you are rejecting yourself. You are saying: 'I'm not good enough or strong enough to do this on my own,' and that becomes a belief which weakens you further because it is false.

Turn away from the voice that says you're not good enough. Teach yourself how to catch negative thoughts as they arise, and then starve them by putting your energy into something that feels good to think about. And, if a negative thought feels good to you, then it's because they're addictive little things. Don't mistake the flash of pain they give you as pleasure.

Negative thinking takes you nowhere positive.

The power you have is the ability in which to choose the direction you want your life to go.

April Green

The good people

Lately, I've been drawn towards the type of kindness you recognise in a person before you even speak to them—it's like an invisible touch that takes you back to remembering that we were designed to be kind.

And maybe we've lost that along the way because we've stopped being kind to ourselves.

April Green

It's in the way you treat yourself

Having a high sense of self-worth is a habit you can learn, and it begins by being kinder to yourself.

Start allowing honey sweet words to run through your bones until they become so natural they sit upon your tongue like starlight.   Watch how everything changes. You are being kind to yourself—you are showing the world that you respect yourself, your body; and the Earth upon which you walk.

You are showing the world that you won't settle for being treated any less than the way you treat yourself.

April Green

fall desperately in love
with the way life is unfolding,
even through the pain.

because one day,
it will all unfold so very

beautifully

April Green

The art of self-love

The times we love ourselves the least are the times we attract the wrong things into our lives the most.

and when it comes—

the healing.
the unfolding of the soul.

let it stay.

April Green

grow

i promise it's not too late
to collect your fallen petals
and start again.

(pick up your abandoned dreams
and fold them, softly, back into
your heart)

April Green

It's never too late to grow

I think that discontentment happens to us when we try to fit into a life we have outgrown. We know it no longer fits; but it's a life we've become accustomed to: it's comfortable, we learn how to tolerate the pain. And instead of stretching and widening our vision, we shrink to fit in, we stay where we are, we stay in the shade.

Without discontentment, we could not grow.

Discontentment, discomfort; that feeling under your skin that you can't quite put into words, is a good thing once you realise that it is a signal urging you to evolve. All you have to do is find something to grow towards, a dream to reach, a wish to hold, *otherwise you will keep settling for where you are.*

Don't let life simply happen to you—take hold of it in both hands and start shaping it into your own vision.

It's never too late to grow.

April Green

Start from where you are

Wherever you are: start from there.

Don't let your mind ever convince you that, just because of your present circumstances, or your past mistakes, you can't change your life by yourself—*you can.* You can rise within yourself. You can create a shift in your vision, change your perspective— think of a wildflower turning towards the light.

You are allowed to get lost every once in a while, (that's how we get stronger), but the door leading towards the better version of yourself has always been open and ready to take you to the next level, (no matter where you currently are in your life). But, remember this: when you take the first step through that door, please don't head towards the person you want to become whilst wearing your current mindset—this will only take you back to exactly where you are. No. Walk towards that person while using their evolved state of mind: think like them, act like them, start to *become* them.

I promise you that in no time at all, you will be walking in their shoes.

April Green

believe

in things that
you can't see.

Know your value

I write to try and make you feel something in case you are numb. In case you are utterly, inadvertently numb through years of avoiding pain; pushing it under your bones like a bad dream in the hope it will be gone by morning. And, in order for me to break something open in you, I have to break something open in me; like a memory, a truth, a fragment of pain we both share. Because, I don't want you to ever feel alone. I don't want you to ever feel like I did: horribly limited in my life because of some untrue belief I'd carved into my bones during the trauma and confusion of growing up.

I want you to know that you can take part in life whenever you decide to. That, even during a (seemingly) endless storm, something will change. Something will awaken inside you and carry you: a desire for more meaning, a desire to create... a role for yourself, a purpose; something that steals your sleep, makes your soul sing with joy.

But, more importantly, I want you to understand that you have a place here; you have a part to play here.

Know your value. Hold it tight inside.

April Green

perspective is... everything:

not all storms are caused by you,
and not all storms are real.

April Green

and i heard her say:

'live the passionate life:

the one that keeps you soft and
breaks you wide open at the same
time.'

April Green

Follow yourself

If you don't yet know who you are or what you want, you will listen to the voices of others, you will follow their footsteps; and you will end up getting lost.

There comes a time when you have to focus solely on your own path, regardless of what anyone else is doing, regardless of what anyone else is thinking. And, I hope that time comes early on in your life. I hope you get to experience the peace and freedom that falls from the sky into your bones when you do what makes you happy. If it feels selfish, then that's a good thing, especially if you are a woman: the moon is always full, it's the shadows that shield her light. Be different. Be focused. Assert your identity. You can achieve whatever you want on your own. Don't you dare wait for the right moment, or the right person. *Bloom for yourself. Always.*

Everything else falls perfectly into place once you learn how to do this.

April Green

your life has a purpose, and
it's in your interest to open yourself up
like a wildflower and connect to that
purpose.

Believe me

If no-one has told you lately that they believe in you, then I'm telling you that I believe in you. But please, start to believe in yourself, because you deserve to have a dream; *and self-belief is the first thing you need to build in order for that dream to come to life.*

You see, it takes a certain kind of strength to believe in yourself; courage to applaud yourself, even just for trying, and very few of us ever do. We don't believe for a second that we are capable of achieving much more than what we're settling for. We spend too much time comparing our lives to the lives of others; too many moments gazing onto their paths, visualising ourselves inside their dreams, that we forget about our own.

You *must* believe that there is a dream for you. But, it won't fall through the sky until you breathe life into it, charge it with the magnetism of desire, claim it as your own.

Start now, exactly where you are. Remove the energy of comparison, and jealousy, and fear; and any other obstacles blocking your dream from reaching you; then take what you already have, (find some light in what you already have) and start from there. Plant some seeds of self-belief and watch them grow by

April Green

focusing on them. Don't you dare look away: self-doubt always visits when you start looking at what other people are doing. Stay where you are, stay on your own path.

Nurture your dream: breathe with it, breathe for it; and it will breathe for you.

my hands are so beautifully

tied

to my dream

Perspective

Try not to think too much about where you currently are—focus instead on where you're going. Because, if you look at where you currently are, then even the slightest touch of doubt, or anger, or comparison, or fear; can hold you there.

But, when you keep an eye on where you're going, then where you currently are is always where you're supposed to be.

Patience is the ability to see your wildest dreams come to life in the present moment.

Flow

When you're happy; you don't look for reasons why other people aren't. When you're secure (in yourself); you don't need approval from others. When you're grateful; you become a magnet for seeing and receiving more things to be grateful for.

You have the capacity to live, and breathe, and grow your own contentment.

So, if you ever find yourself living in someone else's story: ask yourself what it is you're looking for, and then find a way of giving it to yourself.

Self-approval, happiness, joy, are all states of mind that can be attained by living in the present moment.

But, you have to be living in *your* present moment.

April Green

a note:

if you always need approval from others
then you're giving others the power to choose
how you lead your life.

(you're putting your next decision into their hands)

if you can taste it,
(the desire to transform),
then you can speak it
out of yourself—

you can breathe life into it.

April Green

Wisdom from within(ii)

I think you begin to trust your intuitive heart more once you start *acting* upon each message it gives you. Only then do you see how the space opens around you, changes the weight of air.

If you are ever unsure if a message is from the heart, or from the mind, know that the mind sends doubt, the heart sends loving answers, messages, feelings that are always for your highest good. And, sometimes, intuition comes through during a moment of indecision, or fear; or just before something happens that takes your thoughts to, 'I should have listened to myself.'

The heart language is your birthright: it flows around you on a continuous beat, it's what you are born with. It isn't learned, it's what you are given; it's the energy you are created from.

It is the mind that rejects the heart messages. If you allow the mind to take over, then your value becomes diminished because, what you are in fact doing is telling yourself that you don't trust yourself, which translates as: 'you're not good enough.'

The mind is too logical, too heavy, too full of the past

April Green

to ever give you any new answers; it can only give you old answers, old patterns, old behaviours.

Ideas come from inspiration; from the kind of passion that starts inside the heart—something moves it, touches it—a desire from another time, another place, awakens and makes its way to the heart, (always the heart).

That's how your gift finds you. Honour it.

April Green

your individuality is a unique gift:
don't hide it or keep it covered up;
don't leave it untouched.

April Green

The art of passion

Some people are born with creative passion spilling from their veins like shooting stars. From an early age, they know exactly who they are and what they want, and they go and get it. Even when they're held back; they have the courage to rebel, to fight. Art imagines them; it follows them, and they grow into it—they build a life around it.

Other people like me, live, for many years, with the echo of another life pulling at our seams. We rebel, but we don't quite know what we're rebelling against, or fighting for. It's as though something mysterious is trying to communicate with us, as though the cycle of the moon is passing through our bones—half, full, wild, red, pale: the colours of a buried dream—planted for when we understand; for when we're ready.

If you have to wait a lifetime before you're ready: you must let it take your last breath.

April Green

do not be gentle with your dream.

fight for it.

Your passion finds you

If you want to know what your passion is; if you want to know what you are here to do, then I think you should first of all let go of trying to find it, and instead, spend time looking at all the things that are holding it back from finding *you*.

Look at all the things that are resting on top of it; blocking it, holding it down inside you. Look at all the things you're clinging to: the way you want things to be, the way other people are living, the things they have, the things you don't have. Any kind of negativity in your life: anger, jealousy, pain. Anything that feels like a wild sea raging against your bones is resistance, and resistance blocks you from ever hearing the call of your passion.

But once all that resistance is removed, once you are able to start feeling what your soul is drawing you towards, the creative energy within you awakens. It awakens, it expands, manifests itself in many different forms.

This is how your passion finds you. And in the process, you will find a lost language, a stillness that breathes, a gift.

You will find the very reason you were created.

April Green

a kind of soft magic occurs
when you trust the earth to carry you
in the direction of your dreams.

April Green

Inspiration fuels passion

Inspiration finds you when you do something that inspires you. It's reciprocal, a two-way flow; and it's the only way I can describe growing into your passion. It works when you work, because energy flows back to you from wherever *your* energy goes.

And this is how your art evolves: it changes you, it moves you, it expands you to the point of no return.

April Green

one thing i know for certain:

when creativity infuses your heart with its
intoxicating energy, it alters you forever.

Self-doubt kills dreams

Be watchful of self-doubt, for it has a way of suffocating your passion; of holding the soul's desire to create, away from you— far away from you—like galaxies and the sky in between far away.

Whenever self-doubt visits, you must always remember that you are a reflection of the Universe— you were created to create. And, it doesn't matter who else sees your work or likes your work:

the value lies in how you feel when you're producing that work.

April Green

make more art:

it heals

it lives on forever

April Green

the thing about any kind of art,
(writing/drawing/dancing/creating)
is that it allows your true self to speak
without any fear of not being heard.

April Green

i love the art looking back at me, whispering:

'here you are. here. is the relationship. right in front of your eyes.'

love is the bare bones of a poem gazing up at you. it's the broken flowers, the light falling into your hands.

it is everything you love, loving you in return.

when you devote your whole self
to something you do from the soul:

you are alive all the time

Journeys

You are your own teacher—only you know, deep within your heart, what brings you to life; what lights up your eyes like the dust of dancing stars.

And that's all you really need to know in order to live a passionate life.

April Green

The little things

Lately, I have fully understood that until you are grateful for what you already have, you cannot make space for anything greater to enter your life.

It sounds impossible doesn't it? How can I be grateful for this pain or these problems, but the more you focus on them the bigger they grow. So, it's about shifting your focus away from the pain by trying to find joy in the little things.

When you focus your heart, on even the smallest pieces of joy, they will grow.

April Green

Lessons

Everything really does come into your life for a reason: either because it's been designed to fall into your hands to teach you something, (to grow you), or because it's an unlearned lesson returning. If you keep pushing it away, it will keep coming back in a different disguise, because your *unacceptance* of it is creating a magnet which is attracting the same circumstances over and over again.

Start paying attention to *everything* that comes into your life. Try and work out why the same thing keeps appearing; sit with it, untangle it, find out what it wants you to learn. Once you learn, I promise it will stop returning, because you will have cleared the energy. And in clearing the energy, in accepting it for what it is, you will create a space in which to grow.

April Green

at this very moment –
you are being led towards
everything good
that you have asked for

April Green

when you own
every part of who you are.

when you know,
deep within your bones
that your footprints belong
in the exact space you're standing:
like reflections of starlight upon earth

souls find you.

April Green

Love hard

Sometimes, you will find yourself resisting love because you're focusing too much on the past pain of love; and you will end up projecting that pain onto everything good that comes into your life.

But, remember this: love is the only thing on this planet that heals all pain.

If you would just allow the heartbeat of new love, in whatever form it arrives, to connect with your own, it will move you towards a piece of untouched earth. And you will grow.

In one way or another; you will grow.

April Green

allow every new connection
to be woven from the thread
of your healed self.

not from your past story;
       not from the fabric of pain.

April Green

New magic

You can't go into every new connection in life with the fear of losing it—if you cling to the thought of loss, you lose sight of everything coming towards you.

Try and feel every single moment of every new friendship or relationship, as though time's heart is stopping mid-beat for you.

Don't extinguish the magic by thinking about the end before the connection even begins.

April Green

When the soul moves... follow

When you're drawn towards a person because there's something about them that moves your soul—like their openness or their calmness; or the way their eyes sparkle when they talk about something they love—it's because those qualities have awakened the same qualities inside you. Why else would your soul be pulled towards them? It's a recognition, a remembering, an awakening of the parts that are sleeping inside you. They just need to be called upon, embraced, brought into the light.

Become aware that whatever you see in others is always reflecting that which is inside you, because it will help you let go of the traits you dislike and nurture the ones you want to stay. It will help you grow into the person you deserve to become.

April Green

when

souls

find you

let them in

Soul connections

Some people come into your life and you just know, without even thinking about it or labelling it, that there's a special bond; a soul connection: almost as though they're coming back to you.

Honour these connections, however long they last, for they bring with them moments that change the colour of light.

April Green

Souls returning

When a person touches part of your soul, I think their fingerprints stay inside you forever; for I am certain that during moments of extreme emotion, I have felt the same hands brush against me time and time again.

April Green

you draw to yourself
the things that belong to
you.

April Green

A bird in your hand

He taught me about life in the most enchantingly beautiful way:

'It's like holding a bird in your cupped hands,' he said. 'If you hold it too loosely, it will fly away. If you hold it too tightly, it will suffocate. But if you hold it tenderly, lovingly—give it enough space to breathe; you are holding it just right.'

And afterwards, I looked at him and I thought:

'My heart is that bird.'

April Green

Attraction

All those beautiful things we dream about cannot be found in another person until we find them in ourselves first—because it's only when we feel, and become, the very essence of those things, that we attract them into our lives.

April Green

remember:

every given moment,
no matter how ordinary it seems,
is drenched in life, and gaping
with possibility.

moments are *given.*

April Green

Becoming

The space between the life you have and the life you want can be terrifying and overwhelming; but if you embrace the life you have, and the things you can control, then the world you want will start flowing towards you.

April Green

the heart language

it is being honest with yourself, alone;
(every second of the day if you must),
that opens you up to a life beneath the surface.
a life of clarity, and purpose.

a life of undeniable worth.

April Green

finally:

i am more part flowers
than pain.

(nothing has ever tasted so sweet)

April Green

The new life

When you journey into your new life, don't attach any expectations on how you think it should look. Set a goal and create a vision of the person you want to become, but then allow that vision to grow organically; allow it to just be. Things will naturally manifest and fall upon your path, because you have dropped the weight of a hunger for something that never comes; you've dropped the need to control.

The Universe was always showing you the way, you just couldn't see because your focus was directed towards how you thought things should be. But when you drop the need to control, you discover that the Universe really does guide you towards your goals and dreams.

Everything flows very beautifully when you allow it to.

There will still be hurricanes, but they are just passing through, like everything else; let them. There will still be rain; from your eyes, from your heart, from the feelings you are gradually setting free. Let them fall as they need to. There will still be moments of imbalance, and chaos, but if you know where you're going, you will very quickly get back on

April Green

track. Remember to stay on your path: focus on where you're going, keep close the ones who lift you, keep creating, keep building your new life. Stay present. Stay grateful. You will start to attract only those things which are connected in some way to your goal: people, music, signs, messages. Listen. Everything starts guiding you towards your goal, teaches you about patience, and love, and gratitude. The timing is always perfect. You have chosen this new life; you are building it for yourself.

How magical.

April Green

Enjoy the mystery

Once you set a goal, you don't get to choose who or what, falls onto your path; but please believe me when I say that it will always, always be someone, or something, connected to your goal.

The Universe really does work in mysterious ways.

April Green

The people who matter

The people who matter the most are the ones who are there for you the most. They're like those little rays of sunlight that catch the corner of your eye just when you don't think there's any more light left.

Keep them close: absorb every ounce of them, until you are so full of their energy that it has nowhere else to go but back into the space you're sharing.

April Green

a love note:

i can't think of anything more exquisite
than watching a person becoming absorbed
in the thing they are most passionate about.

      (to be lost within the wilderness of yourself
      is the most beautiful place to be)

April Green

Meet yourself in a different light

There must be a million reasons for taking a trip alone, and if you ever do, you'll have a million more. Because, here you are, a world away from home but closer to yourself than you've ever been before.

Sometimes you have to leave the place you feel most comfortable, so you can meet yourself in a different light.

April Green

i hope you learn soon
that the only thing stopping you
from receiving the life you want
is your belief that it's harder than
you think.

April Green

Grow into your dream

You must find a way to allow yourself to grow in the direction of your dream. You must keep shifting your focus from the things you don't want to the things you want. You can't do both: you can't look towards your goal while looking back at the past, it's impossible. If you have asked for something, then it's already somewhere on your path; so you have to keep walking until you reach it.

It's the only way.

April Green

when i think about my past
all i see now is a field of

wildflowers

daily philosophy:

if you do something, (anything),
without being attached to the outcome—

the outcome will always be favourable.

April Green

Grace

Wherever you are, whatever you do, check in with yourself first. Resist the temptation of connecting with the call of the world until you have connected with the call of the wild.

You are in the presence of something very special each time you connect with yourself.

April Green

A final note:

Use defeat and disappointment as a measure of growth, not a measure of worth, or value. Only you can put a value on yourself; no-one else can do that. The only thing other people can do is mirror the value you put upon yourself.

Keep growing, keep blooming.

Understand your own nature completely, and then transform it into something wild and untameable.

Use pain as a message. Use hurt to create— everything can become art, air, poetry, love.

Don't cover yourself up in anyone else's beliefs; become your authentic self again and start from there.

Become all that you are.

April Green

— acknowledgements —

sasha, tina, xavier

&
a very special thank-you to my readers.

your love and support means more to me than you
will ever know.

love,
april green

Instagram and twitter: @loveaprilgreen

follow my instagram blog @bloomforyourself
to read more about healing and self-love.

Made in United States
North Haven, CT
22 February 2022

16371337R00126